The Entrepreneur's Playbook

By

Jeffrey Shane Matthee

Chapter 1. Defining Your Vision.	3
Chapter 2. Validating Your Idea.	12
Chapter 3. Building a Strong Business Model.	24
Chapter 4. Building the Dream Team.	39
Chapter 5. Securing Funding.	55
Chapter 6. Crafting Your Brand Identity.	71
Chapter 7. Sales and Customer Acquisition.	88
Chapter 8. The Art of Scaling.	106
Chapter 9. Managing Finances Like a Pro.	124
Chapter 10. Overcoming Challenges and Building Resilience.	138
Chapter 11. Staying Innovative.	153
Chapter 12. The Exit Strategy.	169
Conclusion.	186
Bonus Sections.	192

Chapter 1

Defining Your Vision

Your Vision Matters

Every successful entrepreneur starts with a clear vision. Your vision is your "North Star"—it guides your decisions, keeps you focused, and inspires others to join your journey. Without it, your business can easily lose direction amidst the challenges and opportunities you'll face.

But a vision is more than just a lofty dream. It's about identifying the impact you want to make in the world and how your business will serve a greater purpose.

The Power of Vision

Real-Life Examples

Elon Musk (Tesla, SpaceX): Musk's vision is to "accelerate the world's transition to sustainable energy" and to "make life multi-planetary." These ambitious goals drive his companies and attract top talent.

Sara Blakely (Spanx): Blakely's vision was simple yet powerful: to empower women by creating more comfortable, flattering undergarments.

Each of these entrepreneurs didn't just focus on a product—they focused on the "why" behind their work.

Crafting Your Vision

Your vision should be:

1. Clear: Avoid vague or generic statements. Be specific about what you want to achieve.

2. Inspiring: It should excite you and others.

3. Actionable: While a vision is aspirational, it should also serve as a practical guide for decision-making.

Exercise

Create Your Vision Statement

Take a moment to reflect on these questions:

1. What problem are you passionate about solving?

Example: "I want to make healthy eating easier for busy professionals."

2. What impact do you want your business to have on the world?

Example: "I want to reduce food waste and make sustainability mainstream."

3. Who are you serving?

Example: "I aim to help environmentally conscious families."

Combine your answers into a single statement.
For instance: "My vision is to create accessible, affordable solutions that reduce food waste while promoting sustainable living for families worldwide."

Aligning Your Vision with Your Values

Your values are the foundation of your vision. They dictate how you'll operate and interact with customers, employees, and partners.

Example Values:

Transparency

Innovation

Sustainability

Community

Exercise: Write down 3–5 core values that are important to you. Ensure your vision aligns with these values.

Bringing Your Vision to Life

A vision doesn't live in your head—it must be communicated clearly and consistently:

1. Write it Down: Post it where you'll see it daily (desk, workspace).

2. Share It: Communicate your vision to your team, investors, and customers.

3. Act On It: Use your vision to guide decisions. When in doubt, ask, "Does this align with my vision?"

Common Pitfalls to Avoid

Being Too Broad: "I want to change the world" sounds great but lacks focus. Narrow it down to something actionable.

Ignoring Your Passion: If your vision doesn't excite you, it won't excite others.

Failing to Adapt: Your vision may evolve over time. Be open to refining it as you learn more about your market and goals.

Conclusion

Defining your vision is the first and most crucial step on your entrepreneurial journey. It's the foundation upon which everything else is built. Take the time to craft a vision that inspires you and aligns with your values. Remember: A strong vision not only sets you apart but also keeps you grounded as you navigate the challenges of building a business.

Next Steps

Take the vision statement you created and share it with someone you trust. Get feedback and refine it until it feels right.

Chapter 2

Validating Your Idea

The Importance of Validation

Having a great idea is only the beginning of your entrepreneurial journey. The real question is: Does your idea solve a real problem for a real audience?

Many startups fail because they skip this critical step. Validation ensures that you're investing time, money, and energy into something people genuinely want and are willing to pay for.

Understanding the Validation Process

Validation involves gathering evidence to prove that your idea is viable in the market. This can be done through:

1. Talking to potential customers.

2. Testing your concept with a small-scale prototype.

3. Analyzing competitors and market trends.

Step 1: Define the Problem

Your idea should solve a specific problem. Start by answering these questions:

What is the problem?

Example: "Busy professionals struggle to find healthy, affordable lunch options."

Who is experiencing this problem?

Example: "Office workers in urban areas."

How urgent or important is the problem to them?

Example: "They're actively searching for convenient meal solutions."

Tip: The more pressing the problem, the easier it will be to find customers.

Step 2: Know Your Audience

Understanding your target audience is key to effective validation. Create a simple customer persona to identify their needs, preferences, and pain points.

Example Persona:

Name: Sarah, 29

Profession: Marketing Manager

Pain Points: Limited lunch options, high costs, lack of time.

Goals: Eat healthy meals without spending too much time or money.

Exercise: Write a brief description of your ideal customer.

Step 3: Test Your Idea

1. Conduct Surveys and Interviews

Create a short survey (5–10 questions) to gather insights.

Example Questions:

What is your biggest challenge with [problem]?

How do you currently solve this problem?

Would you pay for a solution like [your idea]?

Interview potential customers to dive deeper into their needs.

2. Build a Minimum Viable Product (MVP)

An MVP is a simplified version of your product or service that demonstrates its core value.

Examples:

A landing page explaining your product and collecting emails from interested users.

A basic prototype (physical or digital) to test functionality.

3. Test with Real Users

Offer your MVP to a small group of customers.

Observe how they interact with it and gather feedback.

Use this feedback to improve your product.

Step 4: Analyze Competitors

Competitors provide valuable insights into market demand and opportunities for differentiation.

How to Analyze Competitors:

Identify Key Players: Who are the main competitors in your space?

Evaluate Their Strengths and Weaknesses: What are they doing well? What are customers complaining about?

Find Your Unique Value Proposition (UVP): What can you do differently or better?

Example UVP: "Fresh, healthy meals delivered in under 10 minutes."

Step 5: Evaluate Market Trends

Understanding the bigger picture helps you validate your idea further. Look at trends such as:

Changes in consumer behavior.

Emerging technologies in your industry.

Growth rates and market size.

Example: If you're launching a plant-based meal service, you might explore the growing demand for vegan and sustainable food options.

Case Study: A Successful Validation

Startup: Dropbox

Idea: A simple file-sharing service.

Validation Method: The founder created a short explainer video showing how Dropbox would work. It attracted thousands of early adopters before the product even existed, proving demand.

Common Validation Mistakes to Avoid

1. Assuming You Know Your Market: Always test your assumptions with real data.

2. Seeking Validation from Friends and Family: Their feedback is often biased.

3.

4. Skipping the MVP Stage: Developing a full product without testing wastes resources if the idea isn't viable.

Checklist for Validating Your Idea

[ ] Clearly define the problem and target audience.

[ ] Gather feedback through surveys or interviews.

[ ] Develop and test a minimum viable product (MVP).

[ ] Analyze competitors to identify opportunities.

[ ] Research market trends and size.

Conclusion

Validation is about reducing uncertainty and building confidence in your idea. It's better to fail fast and adjust early than to spend months or years on an idea that doesn't resonate with your target audience. By following this structured validation process, you'll set a solid foundation for your startup's success.

Next Steps:

Take your validated idea and start working on your business model, which we'll explore in the next chapter.

Chapter 3

Building a Strong Business Model

What is a Business Model?

A business model is the blueprint of how your startup creates, delivers, and captures value. It's not just about making money—it's about creating a system that sustainably generates revenue while solving a problem for your target audience.

Why a Strong Business Model Matters

Your business model determines whether your startup can:

Generate consistent revenue.

Scale efficiently over time.

Adapt to market changes and stay competitive.

Without a solid business model, even the best ideas can fail.

The Key Components of a Business Model

To build a strong business model, you need to address these critical components:

1. Value Proposition: What unique value does your product or service offer to customers?

Example: "Affordable, plant-based meal kits that can be prepared in under 10 minutes."

2. Customer Segments: Who are your ideal customers? (Revisit Chapter 2 for customer personas.)

Example: Young professionals seeking healthy, time-saving meal options.

3. Channels: How will you deliver your product or service to customers?

Examples: E-commerce website, mobile app, retail stores.

4. Revenue Streams: How will your startup make money?

Examples: Subscription fees, one-time purchases, licensing.

5. Cost Structure: What are your major expenses?

Examples: Production costs, marketing, employee salaries.

6. Key Activities: What are the essential tasks needed to run your business?

Examples: Product development, customer support, logistics.

7. Key Resources: What assets do you need to operate?

Examples: Technology, intellectual property, partnerships.

8. Key Partnerships: Who can help you grow and deliver value?

Examples: Suppliers, distributors, strategic alliances.

9. Customer Relationships: How will you interact with your customers?

Examples: Personalized support, self-service options, community engagement.

Using the Business Model Canvas

The Business Model Canvas is a powerful tool for mapping out your business model. It's a one-page visual framework that helps you organize and refine your ideas.

How to Use the Canvas:

1. Divide a blank page into the nine key components listed above.

2. Brainstorm ideas for each section, starting with your value proposition.

3. Refine your canvas until each element aligns with your vision and market research.

Step-by-Step Guide to Building Your Business Model

Step 1: Identify Your Value Proposition

What problem are you solving for your customers?

Why is your solution better than alternatives?

Example:

Problem: Busy professionals don't have time to cook healthy meals.

Solution: A subscription service that delivers pre-portioned, plant-based meals.

Unique Value: Faster preparation times and lower cost compared to competitors.

Step 2: Understand Your Revenue Streams

Choose the right revenue model for your startup.

Subscription: Customers pay a recurring fee (e.g., Netflix, meal kits).

Freemium: Offer a free basic version with paid upgrades (e.g., Spotify).

One-Time Sales: Sell products/services on a per-transaction basis.

Licensing: Charge for the use of your intellectual property.

Exercise: Write down your primary and secondary revenue streams.

Step 3: Calculate Costs and Pricing

Estimate your costs and set pricing that ensures profitability.

Fixed Costs: Rent, salaries, insurance.

Variable Costs: Raw materials, shipping, marketing campaigns.

Pricing Strategies:

Cost-Plus Pricing: Add a markup to your costs.

Value-Based Pricing: Charge based on the value you deliver to customers.

Example:

If your meal kit costs $5 to produce and you want a 50% profit margin, you'd price it at $10.

Step 4: Develop Your Customer Acquisition Strategy

How will you attract and retain customers?

Marketing Channels: Social media, SEO, email marketing, influencers.

Retention Strategies: Loyalty programs, excellent customer service, personalized offers.

Step 5: Test and Iterate

Your business model isn't static—it will evolve as you gather feedback.

Test different revenue streams, pricing models, and marketing strategies.

Analyze what works and adapt accordingly.

Case Study: Airbnb's Business Model

Value Proposition: Affordable, unique accommodations for travelers.

Customer Segments: Budget-conscious travelers and homeowners looking to earn extra income.

Revenue Stream: Commission on each booking.

Key Activities: Platform development, customer support, and host onboarding.

By leveraging their unique value proposition and scalable revenue model, Airbnb disrupted the traditional hospitality industry.

Common Mistakes to Avoid

1. Ignoring Costs: Underestimating expenses can lead to unsustainable pricing.

2. Overcomplicating Your Model: Focus on simplicity and scalability.

3. Failing to Test: Validate your assumptions with real customers before scaling.

Checklist for Building Your Business Model

[ ] Have you clearly defined your value proposition?

[ ] Do you know who your target customers are?

[ ] Are your revenue streams and cost structures sustainable?

[ ] Have you identified your key resources and activities?

[ ] Is your model simple, scalable, and flexible?

Conclusion

A strong business model is the backbone of your startup. It defines how you'll create and capture value in a sustainable way. Take the time to map out your business model, test it in the real world, and adapt as needed. With this foundation in place, you'll be ready to move forward with confidence.

Next Steps:

Begin outlining your business model using the Business Model Canvas. In the next chapter, we'll dive into assembling a team that can bring your vision to life.

Chapter 4

Building the Dream Team

Why Your Team Matters

Behind every successful startup is a team of driven individuals who believe in the vision and work together to make it a reality. While your idea and leadership are crucial, it's your team that will execute, innovate, and grow your business.

Assembling the right team is one of the most critical steps in your entrepreneurial journey. The people you bring on board will influence everything—from your company culture to your chances of securing funding.

Step 1: Identify the Roles You Need

Start by listing the key roles that are essential for your startup's success. Focus on roles that align with your current stage of development.

Early-Stage Startup Roles:

1. Co-Founder(s):

Shares your vision and brings complementary skills.

Example: If you're a technical founder, look for someone with business or marketing expertise.

2. Product Developer/Engineer:

Responsible for creating and refining your product or service.

3. Marketer:

Handles customer acquisition, branding, and communication strategies.

4. Operations Specialist:

Manages day-to-day activities like logistics, customer support, or finance.

5. Advisor or Mentor:

Offers guidance, expertise, and connections without being a full-time employee.

Exercise: Write down the 3–5 most critical roles for your startup right now.

Step 2: Attract the Right People

Hiring for a startup is different from hiring for an established company. You need individuals who are not only skilled but also adaptable, passionate, and aligned with your mission.

What to Look For:

1. Skills and Experience:

Ensure candidates have the technical or domain expertise required for their role.

2. Cultural Fit:

Do they share your values and vision? Are they excited about the problem your startup is solving?

3. Entrepreneurial Mindset:

Look for team members who are resourceful, proactive, and comfortable with uncertainty.

How to Attract Talent:

Leverage Your Network: Referrals often lead to the best hires.

Use Startup Platforms: Post on platforms like AngelList, LinkedIn, or startup communities.

Offer Equity: If you can't compete on salary, equity shares can attract high-caliber candidates who believe in your vision.

Step 3: Define Roles and Responsibilities

Clarity is essential when building a team. Ambiguity about roles can lead to inefficiencies and conflicts.

Creating a Clear Structure:

Role Descriptions: Write detailed job descriptions outlining key responsibilities.

Decision-Making Authority: Define who has the final say in specific areas.

Shared Goals: Align individual roles with the overall objectives of the business.

Example:

For a product manager:

Responsibilities: Oversee product development, coordinate with engineers, and gather user feedback.

Goals: Launch an MVP within three months.

Step 4: Foster a Positive Team Culture

Culture is the glue that holds your team together, especially during challenging times. As a startup, your culture will evolve naturally, but you can influence it from the start.

Key Elements of a Strong Culture:

1. Transparency:

Share progress, challenges, and goals openly.

2. Collaboration:

Encourage teamwork and open communication.

3. Flexibility:

Allow team members to experiment, fail, and grow.

4. Recognition:

Celebrate wins, no matter how small, to boost morale.

Exercise: Define 3–5 cultural values you want to instill in your startup.

Step 5: Retain and Motivate Your Team

In the fast-paced startup world, retaining top talent can be challenging. Focus on creating an environment where people feel valued and excited to contribute.

Retention Strategies:

Offer Growth Opportunities:

Provide training, mentorship, and chances to take on new responsibilities.

Reward Performance:

Incentivize achievements with bonuses, equity, or promotions.

Build Ownership:

Give team members a sense of ownership in the company's success through stock options or involving them in decision-making.

Common Challenges and How to Overcome Them

1. Conflict Among Team Members:

Address issues early through open communication and mediation.

2. Skill Gaps:

Invest in training or consider hiring freelancers for specific projects.

3. High Turnover:

Focus on building a strong culture and offering competitive benefits.

Case Study: Building Airbnb's Dream Team

In Airbnb's early days, the founders (Brian Chesky, Joe Gebbia, and Nathan Blecharczyk) divided their responsibilities based on their strengths:

Brian focused on design and branding.

Joe handled operations and partnerships.

Nathan took charge of technical development.

They later added team members who specialized in customer support, marketing, and data analytics, enabling the company to scale rapidly.

Checklist for Building Your Dream Team

[ ] Have you identified the key roles you need?

[ ] Are your job descriptions clear and aligned with your goals?

[ ] Do your team members share your vision and values?

[ ] Have you established a culture that promotes collaboration and growth?

[ ] Are you offering incentives to retain top talent?

Conclusion

Your team is your greatest asset. By carefully selecting individuals who align with your vision, defining clear roles, and fostering a strong culture, you'll set the stage for your startup's success. Remember, building a dream team is an ongoing process—adapt as your business grows and evolves.

Next Steps:

Take the time to outline your team structure and start searching for individuals who can fill key roles. In the next chapter, we'll explore how to secure funding to bring your vision to life.

Chapter 5

Securing Funding

Why Funding Matters

Funding is the fuel that powers your startup. Whether it's building your product, hiring a team, or marketing to customers, securing the right amount of funding at the right time is critical for your startup's growth. However, it's not just about the money—it's also about finding the right partners who believe in your vision and can support your journey.

Step 1: Determine Your Funding Needs

Before approaching investors or lenders, you need a clear understanding of how much money you need and why.

Key Questions to Answer:

1. What are your startup's current expenses?

Example: Salaries, office space, product development, marketing.

2. How much runway do you need?

Runway is the time your startup can operate with its current funds. Most startups aim for 12–18 months of runway per funding round.

3. What milestones will this funding help you achieve?

Example: Launching your MVP, acquiring 1,000 users, or scaling operations.

Exercise: Create a budget that outlines your expenses and funding goals for the next 12–18 months.

Step 2: Understand Your Funding Options

There are multiple ways to fund a startup. Choose the one that best fits your business stage and goals.

1. Bootstrapping

Using personal savings or revenue to fund your business.

Ideal for: Founders who want to retain full control and don't need large amounts of capital upfront.

2. Friends and Family

Raising small amounts from people you know.

Ideal for: Early-stage startups with limited access to other funding sources.

3. Angel Investors

Individuals who invest their own money in exchange for equity.

Ideal for: Startups with a clear vision but needing mentorship and early capital.

4. Venture Capital (VC)

Professional firms that invest large amounts in high-growth startups in exchange for equity.

Ideal for: Startups with a scalable business model and significant growth potential.

5. Crowdfunding

Raising money from a large number of people, often through platforms like Kickstarter or Indiegogo.

Ideal for: Startups with a consumer-focused product and a strong story.

6. Loans and Grants

Borrowing money or applying for non-repayable grants.

Ideal for: Startups with predictable revenue streams or businesses in sectors eligible for grants (e.g., tech, green energy).

Step 3: Prepare Your Pitch

Your pitch is your opportunity to convince potential investors or lenders that your startup is worth supporting.

Key Components of a Winning Pitch:

1. The Problem: Start with a compelling description of the problem your startup solves.

2. The Solution: Introduce your product or service and explain how it addresses the problem.

3. Market Opportunity: Highlight the size and growth potential of your target market.

4. Traction: Share any progress you've made (e.g., MVP, early customers, partnerships).

5. Business Model: Explain how you plan to generate revenue and achieve profitability.

6. Team: Showcase your team's expertise and ability to execute.

7. Funding Request: Clearly state how much money you need and what it will be used for.

Exercise: Write a one-minute elevator pitch that captures the essence of your startup.

Step 4: Build a Pitch Deck

A pitch deck is a visual presentation used during investor meetings. It should be clear, concise, and visually appealing.

Slide Outline for Your Pitch Deck:

1. Title Slide: Startup name, tagline, and contact information.

2. Problem: Define the pain point you're addressing.

3. Solution: Explain your product or service.

4. Market Opportunity: Showcase market size and target audience.

5. Business Model: Highlight your revenue streams.

6. Traction: Present key metrics or milestones achieved.

7. Competitive Advantage: Show how you stand out from competitors.

8. Team: Introduce your core team members.

9. Financials: Provide an overview of your projections.

10. Funding Request: Specify the amount and how it will be used.

Step 5: Find the Right Investors

Not all investors are created equal. Look for investors who align with your vision, industry, and stage of growth.

Where to Find Investors:

Angel Networks: Groups of angel investors who pool resources to fund startups.

Venture Capital Firms: Look for VCs that specialize in your industry.

Startup Accelerators: Programs like Y Combinator or Techstars that provide funding, mentorship, and resources.

Networking Events: Pitch competitions, conferences, or local startup meetups.

Step 6: Prepare for Due Diligence

Investors will want to verify your claims and assess the risks before committing. Be prepared to provide:

Financial documents (e.g., income statements, balance sheets).

Customer feedback and testimonials.

Details about your team's background and expertise.

Case Study: How Canva Secured Early Funding

Canva, the graphic design platform, started as a small operation in Australia. To secure funding, founder Melanie Perkins:

1. Clearly articulated Canva's value proposition: democratizing graphic design.

2. Built a strong prototype to demonstrate the platform's potential.

3. Targeted investors who understood the tech space and could provide strategic advice.

This approach led to early funding, which helped Canva scale to a multi-billion-dollar company.

Common Mistakes to Avoid

1. Seeking Too Much Too Soon: Raise only what you need for your next milestone.

2. Failing to Prepare: A lackluster pitch or incomplete financials can turn investors away.

3. Accepting the Wrong Partners: Choose investors who align with your values and vision.

Checklist for Securing Funding

[ ] Have you calculated your funding needs and runway?

[ ] Do you have a clear and compelling pitch?

[ ] Is your pitch deck ready and visually appealing?

[ ] Have you researched and targeted the right investors?

[ ] Are you prepared for due diligence?

Conclusion

Securing funding is a critical milestone for your startup, but it's about more than just money. The right funding partners will provide mentorship, connections, and strategic advice that can propel your business forward. Be strategic, prepared, and persistent, and you'll increase your chances of success.

Next Steps:

Finalize your pitch deck and start reaching out to potential investors. In the next chapter, we'll focus on creating a memorable brand that sets your startup apart from the competition.

Chapter 6

Crafting Your Brand Identity

Why Brand Identity Matters

Your brand is more than just a logo or tagline—it's the emotional connection people have with your business. A strong brand identity helps you:

Stand out in a crowded market.

Build trust and credibility with customers.

Communicate your values and vision effectively.

Whether you're launching a product or a service, crafting a memorable brand identity is essential for long-term success.

Step 1: Define Your Brand's Purpose and Values

Your brand's purpose is the "why" behind your business. It's what drives your mission and resonates with your target audience.

Questions to Answer:

1. Why does your business exist?

Example: "To make sustainable living accessible to everyone."

2. What values define your business?

Example: Transparency, innovation, and inclusivity.

3. What emotions do you want customers to associate with your brand?

Example: Trust, excitement, and empowerment.

Exercise: Write a brand purpose statement that summarizes your mission in one or two sentences.

Step 2: Understand Your Target Audience

Your brand identity should align with the preferences, values, and expectations of your ideal customers.

Steps to Understand Your Audience:

1. Research Demographics: Age, gender, location, income level.

2. Explore Psychographics: Interests, values, and behaviors.

3. Identify Pain Points: What challenges are they facing, and how does your product solve them?

Example Audience Profile:

Name: Emma, 28

Demographics: Urban professional, earning $60,000/year

Pain Points: Lack of time to cook healthy meals

Brand Values She Prefers: Sustainability, convenience, and affordability

Step 3: Develop Your Brand's Visual Identity

Your visual identity is the first impression customers have of your brand. It includes your logo, color palette, typography, and overall design style.

Key Elements of Visual Identity:

1. Logo: A simple, memorable design that represents your brand.

2. Colors: Choose a palette that conveys the right emotions.

Example: Blue for trust, green for sustainability, red for excitement.

3. Typography: Use fonts that align with your brand personality.

Example: Modern sans-serif for innovation; serif fonts for tradition.

4. Imagery: Select photos, illustrations, and graphics that reflect your values and target audience.

Tip: Use tools like Canva or Adobe Express to experiment with logo and design concepts.

Step 4: Create a Consistent Brand Voice

Your brand voice is how you communicate with your audience. It should be consistent across all platforms, including your website, social media, and marketing materials.

How to Define Your Brand Voice:

1. Tone: Decide how formal or casual your communication should be.

2. Personality: Is your brand playful, professional, empathetic, or bold?

3. Key Messages: Identify the phrases or themes you want to reinforce.

Example Brand Voice:

Tone: Friendly and conversational.

Personality: Encouraging and approachable.

Key Message: "Healthy eating made easy for your busy life."

Step 5: Tell Your Brand Story

Storytelling humanizes your brand and makes it relatable. A good brand story explains your "why" and builds emotional connections with your audience.

Structure of a Compelling Brand Story:

1. The Beginning: What inspired you to start this business?

Example: "I struggled to find eco-friendly products that were both affordable and effective."

2. The Problem: What challenge were you trying to solve?

Example: "I realized many people face the same dilemma."

3. The Solution: How does your product or service solve that problem?

Example: "I created a subscription box of eco-friendly household essentials."

Exercise: Write a short paragraph summarizing your brand story.

Step 6: Build Your Online Presence

Your online presence is often the first place customers interact with your brand. It should reflect your brand identity and make it easy for customers to engage with you.

Essential Online Assets:

1. Website: A professional, user-friendly site that showcases your product, story, and values.

Include: About Us page, product/service details, and contact information.

2. Social Media Profiles: Platforms like Instagram, LinkedIn, or Twitter where your audience spends time.

Use consistent visuals and messaging across all platforms.

3. Email Marketing: Build an email list to nurture relationships with customers.

Tip: Use tools like Wix, WordPress, or Squarespace to create your website.

Case Study: Glossier's Brand Identity

Purpose: "Empowering everyone to look and feel like the best version of themselves."

Visual Identity: Soft pastel colors, minimalist packaging, and clean fonts.

Brand Voice: Friendly and inclusive, speaking directly to their audience as peers.

Success: Glossier's strong branding helped it grow into a billion-dollar beauty brand.

Common Mistakes to Avoid

1. Inconsistency: Ensure your brand visuals and messaging are consistent across all platforms.

2. Overcomplicating the Design: Keep it simple and memorable.

3. Ignoring Customer Feedback: Use feedback to refine your brand identity over time.

Checklist for Crafting Your Brand Identity

[ ] Have you defined your brand purpose and values?

[ ] Do you understand your target audience?

[ ] Is your visual identity consistent and appealing?

[ ] Have you developed a clear and authentic brand voice?

[ ] Does your online presence reflect your brand identity?

Conclusion

A strong brand identity is the cornerstone of your startup's success. It sets you apart, builds trust, and fosters loyalty among your customers. By defining your purpose, understanding your audience, and creating consistent visuals and messaging, you'll establish a brand that resonates and endures.

Next Steps:

Start refining your brand visuals and voice. In the next chapter, we'll explore how to acquire your first customers and build lasting relationships with them.

Chapter 7

Sales and Customer Acquisition

Why Customer Acquisition is Key

No matter how great your product or service is, your startup won't succeed without customers. Sales and customer acquisition are about creating a strategy to attract, convert, and retain your target audience. This chapter will help you build a system that drives predictable and sustainable growth.

Step 1: Understand Your Sales Funnel

A sales funnel represents the journey your customers take from discovering your business to making a purchase. It typically includes four stages:

1. Awareness: Potential customers learn about your product or service.

Example: Social media ads, blog posts, or word-of-mouth.

2. Interest: They show interest by visiting your website or signing up for a newsletter.

Example: Free resources, webinars, or product demos.

3. Decision: They consider buying based on your value proposition and pricing.

Example: Reviews, testimonials, or case studies.

4. Action: They make a purchase.

Example: Smooth checkout process and follow-up emails.

Exercise: Map out the journey your ideal customer takes at each stage of the funnel.

Step 2: Identify Customer Acquisition Channels

There are many ways to acquire customers, but not all channels will work for your business. Focus on the ones where your target audience is most active.

Paid Channels:

Social Media Ads: Platforms like Facebook, Instagram, and LinkedIn.

Example: Use targeted ads to promote a new product.

Search Engine Ads: Google Ads for capturing intent-based traffic.

Example: Advertise to users searching for "best meal kits for busy professionals."

Organic Channels:

Content Marketing: Create blog posts, videos, or podcasts that solve your audience's problems.

Example: Write a guide on "5 Quick Recipes for Working Moms."

SEO: Optimize your website to rank higher in search results.

Example: Use keywords like "affordable healthy meals."

Direct Channels:

Email Marketing: Build an email list and nurture leads with valuable content.

Example: Offer a free recipe ebook in exchange for email sign-ups.

Cold Outreach: Reach out directly to potential customers or businesses.

Example: Email restaurants to offer your product as a solution for their needs.

Community Channels:

Referrals: Encourage happy customers to refer friends or colleagues.

Example: Offer discounts or rewards for successful referrals.

Partnerships: Collaborate with complementary brands.

Example: Partner with a fitness app to promote your healthy meal service.

Step 3: Create a Lead Generation System

Generating leads is the process of attracting potential customers who are interested in your product.

How to Generate Leads:

1. Landing Pages: Design dedicated pages that highlight specific offers.

Example: A landing page for a free trial of your product.

2. Lead Magnets: Offer something valuable in exchange for contact information.

Example: Free templates, ebooks, or webinars.

3. Call-to-Actions (CTAs): Use persuasive language to guide users to take the next step.

Example: "Sign Up Now and Get 20% Off Your First Order!"

Step 4: Optimize Your Conversion Rate

Attracting visitors is only half the battle. The next step is to convert them into paying customers.

Tips for Increasing Conversions:

1. Simplify Your Checkout Process: Reduce friction by minimizing steps and offering multiple payment options.

2. Build Trust: Use testimonials, reviews, and trust badges to reassure customers.

3. Use Urgency and Scarcity: Encourage action with limited-time offers or low-stock notifications.

Example: "Only 3 spots left for our VIP subscription—sign up today!"

Step 5: Retain and Upsell Your Customers

Acquiring new customers is costly, but retaining them is far more profitable. Focus on delivering exceptional experiences that keep customers coming back.

Retention Strategies:

Personalized Communication: Send tailored emails based on customer behavior.

Example: "We noticed you loved our meal kit—here's 10% off your next order!"

Loyalty Programs: Reward repeat customers with points, discounts, or exclusive offers.

Example: "Earn 1 point for every $1 spent and unlock free meals!"

Upselling and Cross-Selling: Offer additional products or services that complement their purchase.

Example: "Add our healthy snack bundle to your next order for just $5."

Step 6: Measure and Optimize Your Efforts

To improve your customer acquisition strategy, track key metrics and adjust based on performance.

Key Metrics to Track:

Customer Acquisition Cost (CAC): How much you spend to acquire a customer.

Formula: Total Acquisition Spend ÷ Number of New Customers.

Lifetime Value (LTV): The total revenue you earn from a customer over their lifetime.

Conversion Rate: The percentage of visitors who take the desired action.

Formula: (Conversions ÷ Total Visitors) × 100.

Churn Rate: The percentage of customers who stop using your product.

Tools to Use:

Google Analytics for website traffic.

Email platforms like Mailchimp for open and click rates.

CRM tools like HubSpot or Salesforce for tracking customer interactions.

Case Study: Dollar Shave Club's Customer Acquisition

Dollar Shave Club disrupted the razor market by:

Using Viral Content: Their humorous launch video garnered millions of views.

Simplifying the Process: Customers signed up for a subscription service with a straightforward value proposition.

Retaining Customers: They introduced premium add-ons like shaving cream and wipes, increasing LTV.

Result: Dollar Shave Club built a loyal customer base and was later acquired by Unilever for $1 billion.

Common Mistakes to Avoid

1. Focusing on Too Many Channels: Start with 2–3 channels and master them before expanding.

2. Ignoring Customer Feedback: Listen to your audience to refine your product and messaging.

3. Overlooking Retention: Don't just chase new customers—keep the ones you already have.

Checklist for Customer Acquisition

[ ] Have you mapped out your sales funnel?

[ ] Have you identified the most effective channels for your audience?

[ ] Are your landing pages and CTAs optimized for conversions?

[ ] Do you have a retention strategy in place?

[ ] Are you tracking and analyzing key performance metrics?

Conclusion

Customer acquisition is both an art and a science. By understanding your audience, refining your sales funnel, and building strong relationships, you can create a scalable system that drives growth. Remember, it's not just about getting customers—it's about keeping them happy and turning them into advocates for your brand.

Next Steps:

Identify your top acquisition channels and design a lead generation campaign. In the next chapter, we'll explore how to scale your operations while maintaining quality and efficiency.

Chapter 8

The Art of Scaling

What Does Scaling Mean?

Scaling is about growing your business efficiently while maintaining quality, consistency, and profitability. It's not just about doing more—it's about doing more with the same or fewer resources. Scaling allows you to expand your reach, serve more customers, and increase revenue without overloading your operations.

Step 1: Know When to Scale

Scaling too early can lead to wasted resources, while scaling too late can cause you to miss growth opportunities.

Signs Your Business is Ready to Scale:

1. Consistent Revenue: Your business is generating reliable income and has a stable customer base.

2. Proven Product-Market Fit: Customers love your product and are willing to pay for it.

3. Excess Demand: You're turning away customers or struggling to keep up with demand.

4. Scalable Infrastructure: Your systems and processes can handle increased volume.

Tip: Evaluate your key metrics, such as revenue growth rate, customer acquisition cost (CAC), and profit margins, to determine readiness.

Step 2: Build a Scalable Infrastructure

Before scaling, ensure your business can handle growth without compromising quality.

1. Automate Repetitive Tasks:

Use tools to automate tasks like invoicing, customer support, and marketing.

Example Tools: Zapier, HubSpot, Mailchimp.

2. Invest in Scalable Technology:

Choose platforms that can grow with you, such as cloud-based solutions or flexible CRMs.

3. Standardize Processes:

Document workflows to ensure consistency and efficiency.

Example: Create a checklist for onboarding new employees or customers.

4. Strengthen Supply Chains:

Build relationships with reliable suppliers and ensure you can scale production without delays.

Step 3: Focus on Core Strengths

When scaling, avoid distractions and focus on what sets your business apart.

Questions to Consider:

What is your unique value proposition?

Which products or services drive the most revenue?

Are there any processes or offerings you can streamline or eliminate?

Example:

A startup offering meal kits may choose to focus on their best-selling vegetarian options rather than expanding into multiple cuisines.

Step 4: Expand Your Team

Scaling often requires growing your team to handle increased demand.

How to Expand Strategically:

1. Hire for Key Roles First: Focus on positions that directly impact growth, such as sales, marketing, or operations.

2. Outsource When Possible: Use freelancers or agencies for specialized tasks like graphic design or IT support.

3. Preserve Company Culture: As your team grows, maintain the values and culture that make your business unique.

Tip: Use tools like LinkedIn, AngelList, or remote work platforms to find top talent.

Step 5: Strengthen Your Marketing Efforts

As you scale, you'll need to reach more customers without drastically increasing your customer acquisition cost (CAC).

Strategies to Scale Marketing:

Content Marketing: Publish more high-quality content to attract organic traffic.

Paid Advertising: Increase your ad spend strategically to target new markets.

Partnerships and Affiliates: Collaborate with complementary brands to expand your reach.

Referral Programs: Encourage existing customers to refer new ones with incentives.

Example: Dropbox scaled rapidly by offering free storage space for referrals.

Step 6: Maintain Quality and Customer Experience

One of the biggest risks of scaling is losing the quality and personal touch that made your business successful.

Tips for Maintaining Quality:

1. Hire Customer Support Staff Early: Ensure you can respond quickly to customer inquiries.

2. Monitor Feedback: Use surveys and reviews to identify areas for improvement.

3. Train Your Team: Provide ongoing training to maintain high standards.

Step 7: Expand into New Markets

Scaling often involves reaching new customer segments, industries, or geographies.

How to Identify New Markets:

Customer Data: Analyze your current customer base to find trends and underserved segments.

Market Research: Explore opportunities in different regions or industries.

Pilot Programs: Test your product in a new market before fully committing.

Example: A fitness app originally targeting gym-goers might expand to home workouts for busy parents.

Step 8: Secure Additional Funding

Scaling often requires more capital to invest in technology, marketing, or staff.

Funding Options for Scaling:

Venture capital or angel investors.

Business loans or lines of credit.

Revenue-based financing.

Tip: Create a detailed financial plan to show investors how their funds will drive growth.

Case Study: How Slack Scaled Efficiently

Slack, the workplace communication platform, scaled rapidly by:

Focusing on Early Adopters: Targeting teams in tech and startups who needed better collaboration tools.

Offering a Freemium Model: Attracting users with a free version, then converting them to paid plans.

Investing in Word-of-Mouth Marketing: Delivering an exceptional product experience that users shared organically.

Result: Slack grew from a small team communication tool to a global leader, eventually acquired by Salesforce for $27 billion.

Common Mistakes to Avoid

1. Scaling Too Quickly: Expanding without the necessary infrastructure can lead to poor customer experiences.

2. Ignoring Cash Flow: Ensure you have enough working capital to sustain operations during growth.

3. Losing Focus: Stick to your core strengths and avoid diluting your brand.

Checklist for Scaling Your Startup

[ ] Have you validated that your business is ready to scale?

[ ] Is your infrastructure prepared to handle increased demand?

[ ] Are your processes automated and standardized?

[ ] Have you hired the right people for key roles?

[ ] Are you maintaining quality and customer satisfaction?

[ ] Have you explored and tested new markets?

Conclusion

Scaling your business is an exciting but challenging phase. By focusing on infrastructure, team growth, and maintaining quality, you can expand efficiently while staying true to your vision. Remember, scaling isn't just about growth—it's about sustainable growth.

Next Steps:

Identify areas of your business that need optimization before scaling. In the next chapter, we'll dive into managing finances effectively to ensure long-term profitability.

Chapter 9

Managing Finances Like a Pro

Why Financial Management is Critical

Strong financial management is the backbone of a successful business. It ensures you have the resources to operate, grow, and weather unexpected challenges. Poor financial decisions can sink even the most promising startups, making it essential to master the basics of cash flow, budgeting, and financial planning.

Step 1: Understand Your Key Financial Metrics

Before diving into budgeting or forecasting, familiarize yourself with the financial metrics that provide a snapshot of your business health.

Key Metrics to Track:

1. Revenue: The total income generated by your business.

2. Profit Margin: The percentage of revenue left after expenses.

Formula: (Net Profit ÷ Revenue) × 100.

3. Burn Rate: How quickly your business is spending cash.

Example: If your monthly expenses are $10,000, your burn rate is $10,000/month.

4. Runway: How long your business can operate with its current cash reserves.

Formula: Cash Reserves ÷ Burn Rate.

5. Customer Acquisition Cost (CAC): The cost of acquiring a single customer.

Formula: Total Marketing and Sales Expenses ÷ Number of New Customers.

6. Lifetime Value (LTV): The total revenue a customer generates over their relationship with your business.

Exercise: Calculate these metrics for your business to establish a financial baseline.

Step 2: Create a Budget

A budget is a financial roadmap that outlines your income, expenses, and savings goals.

How to Build a Budget:

1. List Fixed Costs: Rent, salaries, insurance.

2. List Variable Costs: Marketing, production, shipping.

3. Set Revenue Goals: Estimate your income based on past performance or projections.

4. Allocate Funds: Prioritize spending on activities that drive growth.

Example Budget Breakdown:

Marketing: 30%

Product Development: 20%

Operations: 25%

Salaries: 20%

Miscellaneous: 5%

Tip: Use tools like QuickBooks or Wave for budgeting and expense tracking.

Step 3: Manage Cash Flow

Cash flow is the lifeblood of your business. Positive cash flow means you have more money coming in than going out, allowing you to reinvest in growth.

Strategies to Improve Cash Flow:

1. Invoice Promptly: Send invoices immediately and set clear payment terms.

2. Negotiate Payment Terms: Delay payments to suppliers while ensuring customers pay on time.

3. Monitor Inventory: Avoid overstocking to free up cash tied in inventory.

4. Cut Unnecessary Expenses: Regularly review your expenses and eliminate wasteful spending.

Step 4: Build Financial Projections

Financial projections help you plan for the future and demonstrate to investors that your business is viable.

What to Include in Projections:

1. Revenue Forecast: Estimate sales based on growth trends and market data.

2. Expense Forecast: Predict costs for production, marketing, and operations.

3. Profit and Loss Statement: Show expected profitability over the next 12–24 months.

Tip: Be realistic and conservative in your projections to build trust with stakeholders.

Step 5: Plan for Funding Needs

Even if your business is profitable, you may need additional funding to scale.

How to Determine Funding Needs:

1. Calculate how much money you need to reach key milestones.

Example: Launching a new product line or entering a new market.

2. Explore funding options such as venture capital, loans, or grants.

3. Prepare financial documents, including income statements and balance sheets, to present to potential investors.

Step 6: Implement Financial Tools and Systems

Leverage technology to simplify and improve your financial management.

Recommended Tools:

1. Accounting Software: QuickBooks, Xero, or FreshBooks.

2. Expense Tracking: Expensify or Zoho Expense.

3. Payroll Management: Gusto or Paychex.

4. Financial Analysis: Excel or Google Sheets for custom calculations.

Tip: Automate repetitive tasks like invoice generation and expense categorization.

Step 7: Monitor and Adjust Regularly

Financial management isn't a one-time task—it requires ongoing monitoring and adjustments.

How to Stay on Track:

1. Review Monthly Reports: Analyze income, expenses, and cash flow statements.

2. Compare Actuals to Budget: Identify discrepancies and adjust spending as needed.

3. Set Quarterly Goals: Break down your financial goals into manageable milestones.

Case Study: How Buffer Managed Finances Transparently

Buffer, the social media management tool, adopted a transparent financial approach to build trust and accountability.

Public Revenue Dashboard: Shared revenue data publicly to align with their company values.

Regular Financial Reviews: Ensured they stayed within budget while achieving growth goals.

Lean Spending: Focused on prioritizing high-impact investments over flashy expenses.

Result: Buffer scaled sustainably without compromising its values.

Common Mistakes to Avoid

1. Overestimating Revenue: Be conservative in your projections to avoid cash shortfalls.

2. Ignoring Hidden Costs: Account for taxes, maintenance, and unexpected expenses.

3. Delaying Financial Reviews: Regular oversight is critical for staying on track.

Checklist for Managing Finances

[ ] Do you track key financial metrics like revenue, CAC, and LTV?

[ ] Have you created a realistic budget?

[ ] Are you managing cash flow effectively?

[ ] Do you have clear financial projections?

[ ] Are you using tools to automate and streamline financial tasks?

Conclusion

Mastering financial management is essential for ensuring the sustainability and profitability of your business. By understanding your metrics, creating a budget, and planning for the future, you'll have the financial foundation needed to support growth and weather challenges.

Next Steps:

Review your current financial practices and implement any necessary changes. In the next chapter, we'll explore strategies for overcoming challenges and building resilience as an entrepreneur.

Chapter 10

Overcoming Challenges and Building Resilience

The Reality of Entrepreneurship

Entrepreneurship is a journey filled with highs and lows. While the thrill of building a business can be exhilarating, challenges like setbacks, competition, and personal doubts are inevitable. How you handle these obstacles determines your long-term success.

Building resilience—the ability to recover quickly from difficulties—is a critical skill for every entrepreneur.

Step 1: Anticipate Common Challenges

Understanding potential obstacles allows you to prepare and respond proactively.

Common Challenges Entrepreneurs Face:

1. Financial Strain: Cash flow issues, unexpected expenses, or funding gaps.

2. Market Uncertainty: Changing customer preferences, new competitors, or economic shifts.

3. Burnout: Overworking without maintaining a work-life balance.

4. Scaling Problems: Maintaining quality, culture, and operations during rapid growth.

5. Rejection and Failure: Hearing "no" from investors, customers, or partners.

Exercise: Reflect on challenges you've already faced. How did you handle them, and what could you have done differently?

Step 2: Develop a Problem-Solving Mindset

Successful entrepreneurs see challenges as opportunities to learn and innovate.

How to Approach Problems:

1. Stay Calm: Avoid making rash decisions. Take a step back and assess the situation.

2. Break It Down: Identify the root cause of the issue.

Example: If sales are declining, is it due to poor marketing, product issues, or external factors?

3. Brainstorm Solutions: Involve your team to generate creative ideas.

4. Take Action: Choose the best solution and implement it decisively.

Tip: Use tools like a SWOT analysis (Strengths, Weaknesses, Opportunities, Threats) to evaluate your situation.

Step 3: Build a Support Network

You don't have to face challenges alone. A strong network of mentors, peers, and advisors can provide guidance and encouragement.

Ways to Build Your Network:

1. Join Entrepreneurial Communities: Attend events, meetups, or online forums.

2. Find a Mentor: Seek out someone who has navigated similar challenges.

3. Leverage Your Team: Encourage open communication and problem-solving within your company.

Example: Sara Blakely, the founder of Spanx, credits her mentors for helping her navigate tough decisions during her early days.

Step 4: Manage Stress and Avoid Burnout

Burnout is one of the biggest threats to an entrepreneur's productivity and mental health.

Tips to Prevent Burnout:

1. Set Boundaries: Designate work hours and stick to them.

2. Prioritize Self-Care: Make time for exercise, healthy eating, and hobbies.

3. Delegate Tasks: Trust your team to handle responsibilities so you can focus on high-priority activities.

4. Take Breaks: Step away from work periodically to recharge.

Exercise: Identify one activity you can prioritize this week to improve your well-being.

Step 5: Learn from Failure

Failure is a natural part of entrepreneurship, and it often provides the most valuable lessons.

How to Turn Failure into Growth:

1. Analyze What Went Wrong: Look for patterns and identify areas for improvement.

2. Accept Responsibility: Acknowledge your role in the outcome.

3. Adapt and Try Again: Use what you've learned to refine your approach.

Example: Airbnb's founders faced early rejection from investors but used feedback to improve their pitch and ultimately build a billion-dollar company.

Step 6: Build Emotional Resilience

Emotional resilience helps you stay optimistic and focused during tough times.

How to Cultivate Resilience:

1. Practice Gratitude: Focus on what's going well instead of dwelling on setbacks.

2. Stay Connected: Lean on friends, family, or peers for support.

3. Embrace a Growth Mindset: View challenges as opportunities to develop new skills.

Tip: Journaling about your experiences and emotions can provide clarity and reduce stress.

Step 7: Plan for Uncertainty

While you can't predict every challenge, you can prepare for uncertainty by having contingency plans in place.

Steps to Prepare:

1. Build an Emergency Fund: Set aside cash reserves to handle unexpected expenses.

2. Diversify Revenue Streams: Reduce reliance on a single product, customer, or market.

3. Monitor Key Metrics: Regularly review financial and operational data to identify potential risks early.

Example: A retail business might invest in an e-commerce platform to continue operations during economic downturns or pandemics.

Case Study: How Netflix Overcame Challenges

Netflix started as a DVD rental company and faced stiff competition from Blockbuster. Instead of giving up, Netflix:

Pivoted to a streaming model, anticipating the shift to digital.

Invested in original content to differentiate itself.

Focused on customer experience, creating an easy-to-use platform.

Result: Netflix became a global leader in entertainment by adapting to challenges and staying resilient.

Common Mistakes to Avoid

1. Ignoring Problems: Hoping issues will resolve themselves can lead to bigger challenges.

2. Overcommitting: Trying to do too much at once can dilute your focus and resources.

3. Isolating Yourself: Refusing to seek help or advice can make problems feel overwhelming.

Checklist for Overcoming Challenges and Building Resilience

[ ] Have you identified potential challenges your business might face?

[ ] Do you have a problem-solving process in place?

[ ] Are you building a network of mentors and peers?

[ ] Have you implemented strategies to manage stress and prevent burnout?

[ ] Are you prepared to adapt and learn from failure?

Conclusion

Challenges are inevitable in entrepreneurship, but they don't have to define your journey. By developing a problem-solving mindset, cultivating resilience, and preparing for uncertainty, you can navigate obstacles with confidence. Remember, every setback is an opportunity to grow stronger and smarter.

Next Steps:

Reflect on a recent challenge and identify what you learned from it. In the next chapter, we'll discuss how to stay innovative and keep your business competitive in an ever-changing market.

Chapter 11

Staying Innovative

Why Innovation is Essential

Innovation isn't just about creating new products; it's about continuously improving, adapting, and staying ahead of the competition. In today's fast-paced world, businesses that fail to innovate risk becoming irrelevant. Staying innovative ensures your startup remains competitive and continues to deliver value to your customers.

Step 1: Foster a Culture of Innovation

Creating an innovative business starts with building a team and culture that encourages creativity and experimentation.

How to Foster Innovation in Your Team:

1. Encourage Risk-Taking: Allow your team to try new ideas without fear of failure.

Example: Implement a policy where failures are treated as learning opportunities.

2. Promote Collaboration: Break down silos and encourage cross-functional teamwork.

Example: Pair marketing and product teams to brainstorm features customers want.

3. Reward Creativity: Recognize and reward innovative ideas, even if they don't always succeed.

Example: Offer incentives for employees who propose impactful solutions.

Tip: Hold regular brainstorming sessions or hackathons to spark creativity.

Step 2: Listen to Your Customers

Your customers are one of the best sources of innovative ideas. By understanding their needs and pain points, you can identify opportunities for improvement or new offerings.

How to Leverage Customer Insights:

1. Conduct Surveys and Interviews: Ask customers what they love, what frustrates them, and what they wish existed.

2. Monitor Feedback Channels: Pay attention to reviews, social media comments, and support tickets.

3. Use Data Analytics: Analyze customer behavior to uncover trends and opportunities.

Example: Amazon introduced its "1-Click Ordering" feature after identifying customers' desire for a faster checkout process.

Step 3: Stay Ahead of Industry Trends

Keeping up with industry trends ensures you're not just reactive but proactive in shaping the future.

Ways to Stay Informed:

1. Follow Industry Leaders: Subscribe to blogs, podcasts, and newsletters from thought leaders in your field.

2. Attend Conferences and Events: Network with peers and learn about the latest innovations.

3. Join Professional Communities: Participate in forums, LinkedIn groups, or Slack channels relevant to your industry.

Tip: Set aside time each month to review emerging technologies or practices that could impact your business.

Step 4: Embrace Technology

Leveraging technology can streamline operations, improve customer experiences, and open new opportunities.

How to Use Technology to Innovate:

1. Automate Processes: Use tools like Zapier or Salesforce to automate repetitive tasks.

2. Explore AI and Machine Learning: Personalize customer experiences or improve decision-making.

Example: A clothing retailer could use AI to recommend products based on customer preferences.

3. Adopt Emerging Technologies: Experiment with blockchain, IoT, or AR/VR if they align with your industry.

Step 5: Experiment with New Business Models

Sometimes innovation comes from rethinking how you deliver value, not just what you deliver.

Innovative Business Models to Consider:

1. Subscription Models: Offer recurring services instead of one-time purchases.

2. Freemium Models: Provide a free basic version with paid premium features.

3. Platform Models: Create a marketplace that connects buyers and sellers.

Example: Spotify's freemium model allowed it to scale quickly by attracting free users, some of whom later converted to paying subscribers.

Step 6: Collaborate and Partner

Partnering with other businesses can lead to fresh ideas and expanded opportunities.

How to Collaborate Effectively:

1. Find Complementary Partners: Work with businesses that share your values and target similar audiences.

Example: A fitness app could partner with a healthy meal delivery service.

2. Co-Create Products: Develop offerings that leverage both companies' strengths.

3. Share Resources: Collaborate on marketing campaigns, research, or events.

Example: Nike and Apple collaborated to create the Nike+ fitness tracker, combining sportswear and technology.

Step 7: Iterate and Refine

Innovation isn't a one-time event—it's an ongoing process of iteration and improvement.

Steps for Iterative Innovation:

1. Start Small: Test ideas on a small scale to minimize risk.

Example: Launch a beta version of a new feature to a select group of users.

2. Measure Results: Track performance metrics to determine effectiveness.

3. Improve Continuously: Use feedback to refine and enhance your offering.

Tip: Use frameworks like Agile or Lean Startup to implement and test innovations quickly.

Case Study: How Tesla Redefined Innovation

Tesla didn't just build electric cars—it redefined the automotive industry by:

Innovating Product Design: Creating high-performance, aesthetically pleasing electric vehicles.

Embracing Vertical Integration: Building its own batteries and charging infrastructure.

Iterating Quickly: Continuously updating vehicle software to improve performance.

Result: Tesla became a market leader and a symbol of innovation in clean energy and transportation.

Common Mistakes to Avoid

1. Stifling Creativity: Overly rigid processes can discourage innovation.

2. Ignoring Feedback: Failing to listen to customers or employees can lead to missed opportunities.

3. Fearing Failure: Innovation requires experimentation, and not every idea will succeed.

Checklist for Staying Innovative

[ ] Have you created a culture that encourages creativity and risk-taking?

[ ] Are you actively listening to customer feedback?

[ ] Do you stay informed about industry trends and emerging technologies?

[ ] Are you experimenting with new business models or strategies?

[ ] Do you iterate and refine based on data and feedback?

Conclusion

Innovation is the lifeblood of a successful business. By fostering creativity, listening to your customers, and staying ahead of trends, you can ensure your startup remains competitive and continues to deliver value. Remember, innovation is a mindset, not just a process.

Next Steps:

Identify one area of your business where you can experiment with innovation this month. In the final chapter, we'll explore how to prepare for your exit strategy and secure your legacy as an entrepreneur.

Chapter 12:

The Exit Strategy

What is an Exit Strategy?

An exit strategy is a plan for how you'll eventually transition out of your business, whether by selling it, merging with another company, passing it on, or going public. It's not about abandoning your vision—it's about securing the legacy of your hard work and maximizing the value you've created.

An exit strategy isn't just for the end of your journey; it's a roadmap that influences the decisions you make throughout the lifecycle of your business.

Why Plan Your Exit Early?

1. Maximize Value: A well-planned exit allows you to position your business for maximum profitability.

2. Align Goals: Clarify your personal and professional goals, ensuring your exit aligns with them.

3. Prepare for the Unexpected: Even if you don't plan to exit soon, being prepared ensures you're ready for unforeseen circumstances like offers from buyers or changes in the market.

Step 1: Define Your Exit Goals

Start by identifying what you want to achieve through your exit.

Questions to Consider:

What's Your Financial Target? How much money do you need to feel secure?

What's Your Ideal Role Post-Exit? Do you want to remain involved in the company, or are you looking for a clean break?

What's Your Legacy? How do you want your business to be remembered?

Example Goals:

Selling for a specific valuation.

Ensuring your employees and customers are taken care of post-exit.

Step 2: Explore Your Exit Options

There are several ways to exit your business, each with its pros and cons.

1. Acquisition:

Selling your business to another company.

Pros: High payout, quicker process.

Cons: Loss of control, potential cultural misalignment.

2. Mergers:

Combining your company with another to create a larger entity.

Pros: Shared resources, increased market share.

Cons: Complex negotiations, potential integration challenges.

3. Initial Public Offering (IPO):

Selling shares of your company to the public.

Pros: Access to capital, increased brand visibility.

Cons: High costs, regulatory scrutiny, loss of privacy.

4. Management Buyout (MBO):

Selling your business to its current management team.

Pros: Ensures continuity, smoother transition.

Cons: May require seller financing, potentially lower payout.

5. Passing the Business On:

Transferring ownership to a family member or trusted successor.

Pros: Preserves legacy, maintains family involvement.

Cons: Requires finding a capable and willing successor.

Exercise: Identify which exit option aligns best with your goals and business model.

Step 3: Prepare Your Business for Sale

A successful exit requires making your business as attractive as possible to potential buyers or successors.

Steps to Prepare:

1. Streamline Operations: Ensure your processes are well-documented and efficient.

2. Showcase Financial Health:

Have clean, up-to-date financial statements.

Highlight consistent revenue and profitability trends.

3. Build a Strong Brand: A recognizable and trusted brand increases your business's valuation.

4. Develop Key Relationships: Solidify relationships with key customers, suppliers, and partners.

5. Reduce Founder Dependence: Ensure the business can run smoothly without you.

Tip: Hire a financial advisor or business broker to help you navigate this process.

Step 4: Determine Your Business Valuation

Your business's valuation determines how much you'll receive from a sale or transfer.

Methods to Value Your Business:

1. Earnings Multiple: Multiply your annual earnings by an industry-specific multiple.

Example: If your annual profit is $200,000 and the industry multiple is 5, your valuation is $1 million.

2. Discounted Cash Flow (DCF): Estimate future cash flows and discount them to present value.

3. Market Comparables: Compare your business to similar companies that have been sold recently.

Tip: Work with a professional appraiser to get an accurate valuation.

Step 5: Plan the Transition

The transition phase is critical for ensuring a smooth handover to new ownership.

How to Plan a Successful Transition:

1. Communicate Early: Inform employees, partners, and key stakeholders about the transition.

2. Provide Training: Offer guidance to the new owner or management team.

3. Set Clear Timelines: Define key milestones for the handover process.

4. Secure Non-Compete Agreements: Protect the value of your business by agreeing not to compete in the same market.

Example: A founder staying on as an advisor for 12 months to help with the transition.

Step 6: Focus on Post-Exit Goals

Exiting your business is not the end of your entrepreneurial journey—it's the start of a new chapter.

Questions to Consider:

Do you want to start a new venture or take time off?

Are you interested in becoming an investor, mentor, or advisor?

How will you manage the wealth generated from the exit?

Tip: Work with a financial planner to manage your post-exit finances effectively.

Case Study: How Instagram Planned Its Exit

Instagram's founders sold the company to Facebook in 2012 for $1 billion. Their success was attributed to:

Strong Metrics: Rapid user growth and engagement rates.

Streamlined Operations: A small, efficient team.

Clear Vision: A product that aligned with Facebook's goals of expanding its mobile presence.

Result: The founders secured a high payout while ensuring Instagram continued to thrive under new ownership.

Common Mistakes to Avoid

1. Waiting Too Long to Plan: Start planning your exit well in advance to maximize value.

2. Overvaluing Your Business: Be realistic about your valuation to attract serious buyers.

3. Neglecting Stakeholders: Failing to consider employees and customers can damage your reputation.

Checklist for Planning Your Exit Strategy

[ ] Have you defined your exit goals?

[ ] Do you understand the different exit options and their implications?

[ ] Is your business prepared for sale or transition?

[ ] Have you determined an accurate valuation for your business?

[ ] Do you have a clear transition plan in place?

Conclusion

A well-executed exit strategy ensures you leave your business on your terms, whether that means financial freedom, preserving your legacy, or pursuing new opportunities. By planning early and aligning your decisions with your goals, you can make your exit a fulfilling and rewarding milestone.

Next Steps:

Start by defining your exit goals and assessing your business's readiness. Then, explore the best exit option for your situation and begin preparing your transition plan.

Your Entrepreneurial Journey

Congratulations! Reaching the end of this book signifies your commitment to building and scaling a successful startup. Entrepreneurship is a journey filled with challenges, victories, and constant learning. It's not just about launching a business—it's about creating value, solving real problems, and leaving a lasting impact.

As you reflect on what you've learned, remember that there's no single formula for success. Every entrepreneur's path is unique, but the principles outlined in this book provide a strong foundation to guide you through every stage of your journey.

Key Takeaways

1. Start with Vision and Validation:

Your vision is the cornerstone of your business. Take the time to validate your ideas by understanding your audience and solving their problems.

2. Build for Sustainability:

Focus on creating a solid business model, assembling the right team, and managing your finances wisely.

3. Stay Resilient:

Challenges will come, but how you respond defines your success. Embrace failure as a learning opportunity and adapt with a problem-solving mindset.

4. Innovate Continuously:

The market is always evolving, and so should your business. Stay ahead by fostering creativity, listening to your customers, and leveraging technology.

5. Prepare for the Future:

Whether scaling your operations or planning your exit, approach every phase with clarity and intention. Your preparation today sets the stage for tomorrow's success.

Your Next Steps

1. Apply What You've Learned:

Revisit the chapters most relevant to your current stage and take actionable steps. Whether it's refining your business model, expanding your team, or building a strong brand, each step moves you closer to your goals.

2. Stay Curious:

The entrepreneurial landscape is ever-changing. Commit to lifelong learning by staying informed, seeking mentorship, and experimenting with new ideas.

3. Celebrate Small Wins:

Progress, no matter how small, is worth celebrating. Each milestone is a testament to your dedication and hard work.

Final Thoughts

Building a business is not just about profit—it's about passion, purpose, and creating something meaningful. The road ahead may not always be smooth, but it will be rewarding. Remember, you're not alone in this journey. Lean on your network, learn from others, and trust in your ability to adapt and thrive.

As you move forward, let your vision guide you, your values ground you, and your determination fuel you. The future is yours to shape—go build it.

Wishing you all the success in your entrepreneurial journey!

"Entrepreneurship is living a few years of your life like most people won't, so that you can spend the rest of your life like most people can't."

Let this quote remind you that the hard work, sacrifices, and risks you take today are paving the way for a brighter, more fulfilling future. Keep pushing forward, and don't let temporary setbacks stop you from achieving your dreams.

Bonus Sections

Bonus Section 1: Tools and Templates

To simplify your journey, here are practical tools and templates to help you implement the strategies in this book.

1. Business Model Canvas Template:

Map out your business model, including value proposition, revenue streams, and key resources.

2. Pitch Deck Template:

A ready-to-use slide deck for presenting your startup to investors.

Includes sections for problem, solution, market size, and financial projections.

3. Budget Planner:

A spreadsheet template to track your startup's income, expenses, and cash flow.

4. Customer Persona Worksheet:

Create detailed profiles of your target audience, including demographics, pain points, and buying behavior.

5. Sales Funnel Tracker:

A step-by-step guide to track leads, conversions, and customer retention.

Bonus Section 2: Recommended Reading and Resources

Expand your knowledge with these highly recommended books, tools, and platforms:

Books:

1. The Lean Startup by Eric Ries – A guide to building a business through validated learning.

2. Good to Great by Jim Collins – Insights on how companies transition from mediocrity to excellence.

3. Blue Ocean Strategy by W. Chan Kim and Renée Mauborgne – Learn how to create uncontested market spaces.

4. Atomic Habits by James Clear – A deep dive into building habits for personal and professional growth.

Podcasts:

How I Built This by Guy Raz – Stories of entrepreneurs behind some of the world's best-known companies.

The Tim Ferriss Show – Insights on productivity, leadership, and entrepreneurship.

Masters of Scale by Reid Hoffman – Strategies from successful founders and business leaders.

Websites & Tools:

AngelList: A platform to connect with investors and job seekers.

HubSpot CRM: Manage customer relationships and sales pipelines.

Asana/Trello: Project management tools to keep your team organized.

Stripe/PayPal: Payment processing solutions for businesses.

Bonus Section 3: Real-Life Case Studies

Learn from successful startups that followed principles outlined in this book:

1. Airbnb:

Problem Solved: Affordable, convenient accommodations for travelers.

Key Takeaway: Focused on customer feedback to refine their platform and scale globally.

2. Dropbox:

Problem Solved: Simple file sharing and storage for individuals and businesses.

Key Takeaway: Used a viral explainer video to validate demand before building their product.

3. Glossier:

Problem Solved: Beauty products that connect with everyday users.

Key Takeaway: Built a strong brand identity and leveraged social media to drive growth.

Bonus Section 4: FAQs for Aspiring Entrepreneurs

Common Questions and Expert Advice

Q: What if I fail?

A: Failure is a stepping stone to success. Learn from your mistakes, pivot if necessary, and try again with improved strategies.

Q: How do I stand out in a crowded market?

A: Focus on your unique value proposition. Solve a specific problem better than anyone else, and communicate your solution effectively.

Q: How do I balance growth and quality?

A: Invest in processes and systems that scale without compromising customer experience. Prioritize quality even as you expand.

Q: When should I seek funding?

A: Seek funding when you've validated your idea, demonstrated traction, and need capital to reach the next milestone.

Bonus Section 5: Quick Action Plans

For each stage of your business, here's a quick checklist to help you take immediate action:

1. Idea Validation:

Conduct 10 customer interviews.

Build a minimum viable product (MVP).

Test your idea with early adopters.

2. Launching:

Create a detailed business model.

Develop a strong brand identity.

Build your online presence (website and social media).

3. Scaling:

Automate repetitive tasks.

Invest in marketing to acquire more customers.

Hire for critical roles to support growth.

4. Exit Preparation:

Streamline operations and financial records.

Determine your valuation.

Identify potential buyers or successors.

These bonus sections are designed to be your quick reference guide as you progress through your entrepreneurial journey. Whether you're starting out or preparing for an exit, use these tools, resources, and examples to stay focused and inspired.